Genuinely, Genuine

The Story Of Me

Prince,
you have a smile that lights up
a room. may it be a blessing
to you and all those you
come across!
Angela ♥

by Angela Futch

ISBN-10: (1-7352840-0-9)
ISBN-13: 978-1-7352840-0-2

Cover art by Shelley Hickman

Edited by AMF Publishing
Formatted by AMF Publishing

This is for all the dreamers

Never let fear limit you

Inspiration is everywhere

I can't erase your experiences and I can't ignore your feelings

All I can do is understand

All I can do is embrace you along with your humanity

I just ask that you do the same for me and all those you come across

CONTENTS

WELCOME

T　O

M Y

MIND

Penny For My Thoughts?

I want to write, but what is there to say?

I'm searching, but I'm not finding
It's getting harder and harder to be inspired

I want to make people feel
I want to make people think

I want people to question my integrity while they
question their own

I need something to release me, something to
guide me

I'm afraid I'll lose myself before I've even found
myself

Maybe this writing stuff will help...

The poem that started it all...

THE POWER BENEATH YOUR EYES

Your eyes..
Crystal green..
Giving me life..
Giving me hope..

The sun reflects off your eyes, making me feel
more at home than my home itself

Your eyes allow me to feel love
True and genuine love
Love that could last a lifetime

Love that evolved from one sided feelings on the
playground to mutual love and respect for one
another

You know the love is real when the universe pulls
you together time and time again

Separated from one another, but always feeling
close

It started when we were kids,

Your eyes brought us together that day by the stairs

Your aura floated towards mine cause it knew we needed each other

I'm grateful everyday because without your eyes,

I'd still be lost

To Be Poetically Anxious...

Fear of Self

For a while, I was struggling

I was consumed with thoughts of absurdity

I hated how I was losing sight of reality

I hated how I was losing my sense of purpose

But most of all,

I hated feeling hopeless...

The Rabbit Hole

I'm the only one here and it's so dark
It feels like I'm falling in slow motion

I scare myself into silence
I keep myself company by overthinking

The anxiety takes my humanity away
I try to fix it, I try to fix myself

I don't want to burden anyone so I shut down
Autopilot has been switched on

I'm no longer in control

TRAPPED

So much depends upon how I'm feeling that day

How fast is my head spinning?
How many times have I already forced a smile?
How many times have I said I was ok, but I really
wasn't?

When you ask me what's wrong, you remind me
that I'm trapped in the rabbit hole

I know you're just trying to help, but that makes it
worse

I don't know what's wrong
I can't seem to escape my mind

And so,

I fall deeper into the rabbit hole

Thoughts From the Rabbit Hole

How will they react if I say this?
Maybe if I smile they won't ask if I'm okay

Will they feel uncomfortable if I do this?
I don't want to make them to go out of their way

Why am I constantly at war with my mind?
I don't know what's real anymore

Who will stick around if I keep doing this to myself?
They will grow tired of wiping my tears that fall
aimlessly

Why do I always need reassurance?
Nothing traumatic has ever happened to me

Did I really just run a red light?
Maybe if I laugh it off, Alyssa won't say anything

Why do I try to escape the darkness when I know
I'll never make it out

E   M   P   T   Y

it's like all the oceans dried up

and all the stars fell out of the sky

i don't know where this comes from

i pray that it's only temporary

but it never goes away

this emptiness,

it is always here

consuming my mind

I'M SORRY

There's so much going on inside my head,
everything goes by like a blur

My life feels like a dream, but it's not a happy
dream

It feels like I'm falling, falling into a black abyss

Please take my hand and pull me out,
but not if you'll lose yourself in the process

I can't ask you to save me when you need to save
yourself..

I'm sorry I make everything so difficult

I'M TRYING TO ESCAPE

I want more for myself, but I don't know how to strive

I want to be happy, but the joy is fleeting

When I question why I feel this way, nothing comes to mind

I'm finding it harder and harder to be in the present moment

I hate feeling like this when I know I'm destined for something great

what am i to do?

the song plays

the tears roll down my face

when i think, my mind goes crazy

i don't know where this sadness comes from

i can't explain it,

i wish you could read my mind

what am i to do

when i'm the one destroying myself?

LOST

I try not to complain because everything in my life

has always been good

People have gone through so much worse

Who am I to ask for help?

Life is a puzzle that makes me question everything

I can't seem to make the pieces fit

Sadly it seems as though

I am my own worst enemy

Hope From the Rabbit Hole

I'm losing sight of my desires and my passions

I don't want to live without a purpose
I don't want to live in the sea of worry that is my
mind

I need to face the bad, so the good will be even
greater

What am I running away from?

One day I'll find a way to create a happiness that is
everlasting

One day,

I'll No Longer Fear Myself

To the one who loved me through it all...

Fear That You'll Leave

Even platonic love can be confusing

Sometimes it can feel like romantic love

Other times it can feel like the thing you needed most

This is a story of doubt and a story of reassurance

This is a story of unconditional love...

The Intricacies of Love

I know you love me, but
Do you love me as much as I love you?

This is what I ask myself instead of being in the
moment with you

I know I can't change you,
I just want to feel that my love is reciprocated

I doubt everything and it's not fair to either of us

I hope you know,
I mean it the most when I tell you I love you

All you've ever done is shown me kindness and an
open heart

Who am I to ask for more?

JOURNEY GUIDE

You got me thinking
Could something really be there?

No, there can't be
I haven't thought this way in years

Well.......maybe in the back of my mind it lingers

I guess that's love in its craziest form

I love him so much, I question if I'm in love
I love him so much I don't care that he might not
love me the same in return

He affects me in the deepest, scariest ways
He guides me through life, giving me hope and
inspiration

I always resort back to him
He's been the most constant thing in my life, saving
me from myself and those around me

But..

Who's going to save me from him?

CONFLICTED

Why is every poem about you?

I'm not mad, you are worthy

I'm just conflicted..

the reciprocation i always wanted

you are Home
you are Comfort
you are Freedom

i wish I knew how to help you, but i don't

my past doesn't allow me to show love the way you
need it, but that doesn't mean my feelings are any
less valid

when you feel like my love isn't enough,
know that you are the first person i've ever truly
loved

you will Always be loved by me

Imagination vs. Reality

You were patient when I didn't allow myself to be
loved

You filled the hole that had been empty my entire
life, the hole that was dug deeper and deeper by
people who claimed to love me but did not

Unexpectedly you changed my life
Grateful and blessed are an understatement

Words only need to be said because I need
reassurance, but you understand that

I imagine a world where I finally have meaningful
relationships, but when it comes to you

It is no longer my imagination,

It is my reality

NOTED

You hate the way the sand lingers between your
toes after a day at the beach, while I live for it

You never know what to say, while I always find the
words..

We're so similar, but so different
It's beautiful

You glide through life one way and I float through
life in another

You were the first to stick around
Because of you, I am a better person

Because of you,

I've grown accustomed to unconditional love

The First Time I Saw You

I remember it like it was yesterday..

I was walking towards the staircase and you were
smiling at the person talking to you

Your turned your head to the left and that's when I
saw the most beautiful green eyes

At that moment, I was transfixed

No, not because you were the cutest kid at school,
but because you had this way about yourself

You stood with your shoulders rolled back and
your head held high

I picked up on your energy before I even knew
what energy was

You were so young, but already so wise

You were calm
even when the chaos surrounded you

The first time I saw you, I knew right away that you
would be a part of my life

I no longer fear that you'll leave me
I finally get it now..

You could never leave me because

You Were The One Who Loved Me Through It All

Love oh Love, what are you...

Fear of Deception

If I love

will I be enough?

will I watch myself fade away?

or will my flaws you once adored destroy you?

in LOVE with the idea

i step away from reality
my departure will not be missed

anyone who intrigues me becomes an escape
the possibilities are endless

it takes one transfer of energy
i dive into the next series of fantasized love stories

you are now the subject of all my thoughts

Disease or Paradise

Love is scary because it can be a disease or a
paradise, toxic or healing

We take that chance when we allow those feelings
to flow, heading into the world of the unknown

Love could be angelic

if

only

it

were

real

TRUST THE JOURNEY

I've been trying to figure out how to tell you this, so
that you see what I see

Know that I'm not judging you for wanting
someone, we all just want to be loved

But you see, love shouldn't be forced

Love begins with interest
Then that interest blossoms into passion and that
passion leads to commitment

Love doesn't happen when you want it, love
happens when you least expect it

You must understand that the things that happen
to us when we're young, shape who we are when
we're older

Dig deep and find what makes you happy

Maybe the universe hasn't sent you a lover because
you're not ready yet

Maybe if you stopped looking for love, love would
find you

You must search for yourself before you search for love

Be content with where you're at in life because the journey of love only complicates things

You need to believe that you are so undeniably amazing, that anyone who cannot see past your outer layer is not worthy of your time

Do not waste your time on immaturity and forced feelings, love will come to you

Trust the journey

And one day someone will be in love with you, the way I love you

L-O-V-E

Love is exploring without fear
Love is seeing without a clouded lens

Love is passion when the spark dies down and the
honeymoon phase is gone
Love is communication when the kids won't stop
fighting and the rent needs to be paid

Love is stacking your plates for the busboy
Love is throwing twenties instead of throwing ones
Love is being kind to those that have wronged you

Love is dancing to the heartbeats of those who
came before us and singing songs for those who
will come after

Love is creating worlds you never thought were
possible

Love is being yourself and cherishing every minute
Love is observing the world and wanting to heal it

Don't you see,

Love Is Only Deception If You Allow Yourself To Be
Deceived

To love in silence...

Fear of What She'll Think

She came into my life

I explored my identity

I explored my sexuality

I was changed forever...

Photograph

My eyes always found her

She was the first thing I saw, the first person I took
in and admired

I could never look away

She was effortlessly beautiful, effortlessly alluring

My world stopped for her and her only

Oh, to be fixated

I was so aware of her leg brushing against mine

She wore khaki shorts and a white t-shirt, both
hugged her in all the best places

The sun enhanced the golden specks in her left eye

She brought the fork to her mouth like an angel

That french toast was blessed to have touched her
lips

If only she knew,

I was in awe of everything she did

The Beauty of Fixation

She made me feel like a kid in a candy store

I was fixated on the infinite wonders beneath her
surface

She was all I ever wanted..

I was finally seeing in color

That One Justin Timberlake Song

This song speaks of the things I wanted to tell her
all those times I walked her to class

I hear the first 2 seconds and I'm ready to feel
monumental again

The chorus comes and I laugh
I laugh because I used to sing her name like she
was mine

If I ever got the chance,
I'd show her this song and I'd say

*When I hear this, it makes me think that maybe we
were meant to be..*

Meant to Be

If we were meant to be, our love would be the fairytale I always wanted, but told myself I'd never get to have

You would be my queen and I'd follow you wherever you wanted to go

Into the enchanted forest or down the yellow brick road

I'd follow as long as you were there

to Her future lover

Tell her everyday that she is stunning
Cherish every moment with her

Remind her that her capabilities are endless

Make sure she never loses the peace she was
searching for in the hallways at Gunderson

Love her so hard that she is always smiling
Love her like there's no tomorrow

Love her the way I never got a chance to

T. F. F.

Any mention of her knocks me on my ass
It's been two years and she still affects every part
of me

My mind.   My body.   My soul.

She was monumental, so showing her love was easy
Being around her felt like a necessity

If I ever got the chance, I'd say to her

You changed me
The way I think, the way I feel
The way I move through this world

How could I fear what you think when

Loving You In Silence Was One Of The Bravest
Things I've Ever Done

I think I'll write in code...

Fear of Exposure

The moment she spoke, I was captivated

I couldn't stop writing about her

She watched me put these words on paper

Little did she know, every word was for her...

RANGER

It's the way your face lights up when you talk, I
hold on to every word you say

I ask you questions I already know the answer to,
just to hear you speak

Your voice is lyrical
Your laugh is heavenly

You live life with ease, I don't want to miss out
I want to earn your respect, not your fondness

I wonder what you dream of
I wonder who you are when no one's around

I am so intrigued,

Please let me learn from you

CAPTIVATE

Locking eyes with you is an all encompassing experience

You are an angel in hell, the light in the dark

Please enlighten me, bring me back to life

Teach me how to hold that much strength in only my eyes

Teach me how to captivate the way you've captivated me

PEARS

While I watch you eat your pears, I have this
sudden urge to try some

It's funny how things work..

Here I am, craving this awkwardly textured fruit
that I've never liked before

Here I am, writing another poem about you that
you'll probably never see

I THINK I LIKE PEARS NOW

Come learn life with me

We'll dance with the waves
and journey through national parks

I don't want to write in code anymore
I want to scream your name as loud as I can

To have you would be worth the exposure

MARVELOUS MARY

I have found my very own Mary
All I want to do is eat pears and walk in the forest
holding your hand

I can't sleep
I'm in a trance writing about you
I'm creating a reality where you and I are side by
side

You are so marvelous, I don't care if nothing comes
of this

I don't care if i'm making it all up

You will do far greater things than I..

I was just lucky enough to experience you before
you rose above us all

HEAVENLY

You and me Ranger..

We could be a powerful force of butterflies and

waves taking on the world

Gracefully superior you are..

You float through life effortlessly like a butterfly

safe in a national park

BATHROOM CONCURRENCES

When I saw you
everything else disappeared

And for a split, blissful second
all that remained was you standing there

Smiling at me

THE PRESENCE OF YOU

The words come so easily when I write about you
I experience you in small doses that only make me
want more

Your smile is warm
Your presence is bright

Please stay forever

FLOAT LIKE A BUTTERFLY

You are beautiful

Do not hide your intelligence

You are smarter than everyone here

Let your thoughts go

Float like a butterfly

CRASH LIKE A WAVE

Oh Ranger, why can't you stay longer?

Why do all the best people in my life feel
temporary?

I don't need to be a wave anymore

I'll be a butterfly if it means I can be with you

GOODBYE RANGER

I refuse to knock you off your wavelength

I don't want to disrupt what you've already
imagined for yourself

I wrote these poems in code, so I could preserve
the serenity you gave me

I'm happy to say,

I'm No Longer Afraid Of Being Exposed

To the one who brought the light...

Fear of Losing the Light

I hope everyone is lucky enough to come across a
person who lights up a room with just their smile

Their presence is freeing and they cannot be hated
because it is in their being to spread joy

These people are rare, so if you find them, hold on
tight

Sometimes they may have to leave, but you will find
that their light still remains...

A Poem for the Light

When you were here, life was exceptional

Everyone around you was able to live fearlessly

You showed us the power of being so full of joy that
it's contagious

Your light spans the globe

It is in us all

A Love Across The Atlantic

on the way to the room, her steps become lighter

she knows he's there, so she's eager to go in

she can't help but be happy when she's around him

her eyes find him when she walks into the room

her spirit is floating, floating towards his

it seems as though their hearts are intertwined

their connection runs deep, deep like the sea

they will always share a love across the atlantic

oh, how lucky i was to witness this great love

this love that will stand the test of time

The Light Remains

Your light is in the sparkle of her eye when your
name is mentioned

It's in the grass where we talked for hours
It's in the music that plays when I drive

I could never lose you,

Your Light Will Always Be With Me

When lust is confused for love...

Fear of Lust

I was stuck playing a dangerous game

I was pulled back and forth for so long

Never again will I confuse lust for love...

an ineffable feeling

at that moment when i made you laugh,

you held me tighter and brought our bodies closer

it felt like our souls were aligned,

like we were supposed to stay like that forever

love or lust?

if i could,

i'd drive over to your house just to hug you

when it was time to let go,

i'd hold on a little longer and a little tighter

i'd hold you so close,

your energy would pass through me and i'd be a

part of you

I think it's just lust

i wonder why i stick around
this often feels pointless

when we go our separate ways
things seem to fall apart

i've written so many fucking poems
i'm tired of getting nowhere

this doesn't feel right
and yet

i keep coming back

a different type of ineffable

you walked right in front of my car and said
nothing

i watched you ignore my existence

that moment summed up our entire relationship..
a relationship that only existed in parked cars after
the sun had set because to you that was enough

but that will never be enough for me

i finally realized
it wasn't me, it was you

only you had the power to let others love you

you played yourself

you told me we shouldn't have sex because i would want someone to stick around afterwards..

you said that like you were planning on leaving after, like you were planning on walking out of my life again..

i always knew we would never be anything more than a parked car convo

it was definitely just lust

you will never get another private dancing party

you will never get to hear another poem
you will never get to call me a friend
you will never get to touch me

i was always honest with you
i was ready to give myself to you
i was ready to be with you in every way

silly you, i would've moved mountains for you

caught in the idea of love

boy was i delusional
i didn't love you

i loved having all the attention on me
i loved exploring myself through you

i loved being touched

lesson learned

my days are good without you

you were never meant to be a friend
or a lover

you were simply

a lesson to be learned

an untold story

january 28th, 2020, *love* slipped from your mouth
and made its way to my ears..

ha! what a fucking atrocity

let's be real,
you were having an identity crisis while i was too
scared to say what i wanted

i went back all those times your actions didn't
match your words because i thought i was what
you needed

but that's the thing,

i was never going to be enough for you
because you weren't enough for yourself

you asked me not to speak of us unless we were
the only ones present

i tried, i really did

i tried to keep us a secret even when it didn't feel
right

i couldn't find the strength to tell you that
it's in my being to share my happiness with those
around me

i should've told you from the jump that i really only
wanted you for one reason

at the time, neither of us were seeing with clarity
we were both unable to free ourselves from the
cycle

i was using you, but you were using me too
we wanted the things that brought out the worst in
each other

we played each other and we played ourselves

you can only blame you

and

i can only blame me

goodbye mr. gooday

you said so many things that never came true
you walked out of my life too many times

i have to admit, i was hurt
i was ready to be petty and immature

i wanted you to feel what i felt all those times your
actions betrayed your words

i almost convinced myself that i needed to make
sure we were on good terms

but for what?
so you could avoid me at school like you weren't
fantasizing about me the night before?

you continued to leave, while i continued to try
because that's what i do

i love people even when they don't deserve it

i love people even when they aren't ready to be
loved

but unlike you, i can own up to my feelings

i can say that i still think about our past
i can say that i wrongfully used you

and i can also say goodbye
goodbye to you and your baggage

i hope one day you conquer your fears that stop
you from trusting yourself because

I No Longer Fear Lust

Thoughts for my future lover...

Fear of Being Alone

I like to imagine the romance I desire

In my fantasy, my lover inspires me

They challenge me and they expand my mind

Only time will tell if this fantasy becomes a reality...

Marvelous

You told me never to hide my true emotions

You told me I wasn't bound to this planet

You told me I needed to live unapologetically, in

the biggest and loudest ways possible

You told me never to fabricate a list of nothings

when everything I am is marvelous

Tell Me You Love Me

I want to be with you every minute

There aren't enough seconds in the day

You make me mad, you make me sad, you make me

happy, so undeniably happy

I don't want to scare you, but I'm scared for myself

Reassurance is a necessity from all the past times

people have left

Please be patient and tell me you love me

Oh, to be in love

I love you more than I love watching Frasier

I love you more than the way I feel when I dance

I love you more than writing because nothing is
falsified when it comes to you

The love I always dreamt about is finally here, right
by my side

A Poem For My Future Lover

I loved you before I even knew you

Everyday I'll tell you the story of my love

I promise to create worlds for you

I believe in you and I believe in us

The time has finally come for me to fall in love,

I Will Never Be Alone Again

Poems to everyone and no one...

Seeing Through Fear

Everyday we have to choose to live fearlessly

Because at any moment, darkness can find its way in

I believe negative feelings are inevitable, but whether

or not we continue to feel them is up to us

I'm only beginning to understand this power that I

have...

DROWNING

My favorite place was floating in the waves
alongside you, hand in hand, bare skin to bare skin

We held each other and let the waves rock us into
bliss, peace and satisfaction arose in us both

We were reminded that we're so small in this
world, but our impact could've been as great as we
wanted it to be

Together we could have built a love that ran as
deep as the oceans

Together we could have built a love that was
stronger than the seas most powerful waves

Too bad you let me go,
the current came along and you got scared

As I was taken under by the force, water filling my
lungs, I realized I was losing you

I opened my eyes to see if I was okay,
but there was no sunlight

You were the light that lit up my life and when you let me go, I went dark

You see, drowning was what it felt like to lose you

And the worst part about it was, you left me because I wasn't enough for you

That's what it feels like when you lose someone and it's your fault

D R O W N I N G

You have no control over it,
you are dragged slowly into the dark abyss,

Alone and stripped of everything because you gave it all to the person that let you go when the current came along

AMBIVALENCE

Our car rides are getting quieter
It's like there's nothing left to say

We went from talking about three different things
at once, to not talking at all

Looking back, it seems like nothing ever made
sense when it came to you

I used to think I didn't know who I was without
you, but I'm aware of how dangerous that
sentiment is

I used to be so open around you,
I could say anything and everything

Now you feel unfamiliar
I sit back and watch you live a life I feel I'm no
longer a part of

It's like all the years I've spent with you have been
erased

I wanted you to be someone you were never
capable of being

You were a figment of my imagination and I was
fooling myself the entire time

Maybe we got caught going through the motions
and there isn't anything more we can do

I miss you, I really miss you
I feel nothing and everything at the same time

I don't want to lose you,
but I don't want to fight for you either

ORION'S BELT

You keep everything in and only torture yourself
more

I don't think you see how much I can do for you
because I see how much you can do for me

I have good days and I have bad days,
but with you they could all be good days

The universe is telling me that you are the key,
but how do I know if you'll fit into my lock

I don't know if you're truly different or if I'm using
you as a distraction to save me from this lost
feeling that I have

You ask me why I feel lost and I want to tell you all
the complicated long stories and details

You say you'll be there, but I don't think you realize
that it's so much deeper than that

Please heal me,

Save me and I'll do the same for you

REVELATION

Enough of this *poor me* shit

I don't need validation from anyone

I won't allow myself to fear the unknown

I understand that I'm the only thing that I can

control

I won't let my mind consume me

I will find a way out of the rabbit hole

A DIAMOND OF DIRT

I have spent so much time at this place

I used to love every part of being here
I used to laugh with my shitty teammates
I used to look forward to the hot weekends spent
in the middle of nowhere

I have laid myself down literally and metaphorically

But the dirt between my nails is now a bother..
The pebbles that find their way into my pants no
longer satisfy me, they make me feel trapped

I'm not fulfilled like I once was
How does passion up and disappear?

It feels like I'll have to reinvent myself if I stop
playing

Who will I be if I walk away?
Who will I be if I'm not an athlete?

I hate feeling like I'm obligated to play
I don't want to abandon my teammates, but I can't
keep doing this to myself

I wasn't put on this Earth to be a softball player, I
was put on this Earth to love

I was destined to be a dreamer and I no longer
dream of softball

I think it's finally the time to say goodbye to this
diamond of dirt

A California Sky

The sky reminds me of the times we drove,
windows rolled down with the music blasting

We watched the sky change colors and talked for
hours under the stars

I called you
I wished you a happy birthday
I sent you songs even when you didn't say a word
to me

I welcomed you into the intricacies of my life, but
you still left me hanging

Honestly,
I'm not surprised that this happened

I'm not surprised your immaturity clouded your
judgement and blinded you from seeing the friend
you had in me

I see that you were only meant to be in my life temporarily

You showed me that I can only do so much

I can't force someone to be my friend and I can't make someone give me closure

I didn't lose you, you lost me
You are just a friend I used to have

My happiness no longer involves you

dreaming of Her

she was working at a Best Buy

i couldn't believe it was Her

she was flirting with the girl behind the counter

boy, was I happy to see them talking like that, it
meant i had a chance

if she could flirt with that girl, she could flirt with
me..

i woke up with a smile on my face

a happy poem on a Gooday

do you remember on that first night when you

played a song by The Weekend?

i told you i didn't really like his music

you were appalled and I laughed

that moment made me feel prevalent..

the music always brought us together,

it was the only real thing we shared

it made the moments i spent with you feel infinite

SoCal Boy

You smile with your whole body
Your eyes squint and your brows furrow down as
your body sways back and forth

It is a smile that warms an entire room

Whenever we part ways, I always feel like I'm losing
something

Isn't that crazy?

My time with you is always fleeting,
but when I'm by your side, I feel like I can be
brighter than I already am

HEY ROOMIE

I remember the exact day I met you

All it took was an hour and I knew you were unlike
anyone I had ever met before

We only had three weeks together, but those were
the best weeks of my life

I finally met someone who could teach me more
than I could teach them

I think of you at random and it puts my mind at
ease

Know that my spirit misses you and that you are
one of the best things that could've happened to
me

Everyday,

I cherish your existence

Dear Younger Self

You are valuable

Your words matter

Your purpose in life is not to hold a glove and a bat

You are not just a pointless conversation next to

those big green plants

Sometimes you will have to let people go because

they cannot help themselves

One day you will love yourself so much that you

can't help but share your love with the world

In Loving Memory of a Marine Biologist

My love for the ocean is the only thing that has
always been there for me

I never grow tired of it, it is the perfect friend

Isn't it beautiful, the way it moves
The way it gives and gives and gets nothing in
return

We depend on it so much and we're not even aware

We're ignorant to its power, ignorant to its effect
and what life would be if it were gone

There is no life without the ocean

I am nothing without the sea

Ya Feel Me

I'm the type of person who is fascinated by life and
everything it has to offer

I sit outside and wonder what the birds say to each
other

I turn off the lights during the day because the
sun's light feeds my soul

I read books because they take me to other worlds,
worlds I hope to create one day

I walk in public and look at as many people as
possible because everyone has something to offer,
even if it's just a smile

Often times, I don't see the point in sitting in a
room full of people staring at their phones

I'm all about good vibes and good energy, so if we're not feeling the same way, then I would rather not waste my time or your's

I've come to realize that my intricacy is a luxury

If you can't hang,

Get to steppin

My Love

Love like this doesn't need to be justified or

explained

I'm not crazy for feeling this way, I am human

If I didn't love like this, I wouldn't be me

I won't let the best thing about me get twisted into

a burden or a sin

My love is freeing

THE BEST TYPE OF SELFISHNESS

Do not compare yourself to others

Simply, be you beautifully

Love others openly and love yourself entirely

Show endless compassion, but expect little from

others

Reveal yourself to people even when they don't

deserve it

You will find you are free

because you are happy, peacefully and entirely

happy

A DREAMER

You are not what your parents say you are
You are an artist

It's not a bad thing if you want to be difficult to
understand

You're unlike anyone else
Only those worthy will be able to see that

You are a believer in humanity, a believer in a
creator who preaches compassion

Your intricacy is undeniable

One day soon you'll proclaim your message and
everyone will receive it and be changed

I'm looking forward to reminiscing on the times we
spent feeling divine

Late night talks turned into early morning reflections

We reminded each other that our existence is monumental

I believe in you like I believe the sun will rise tomorrow

Always remember,

Dreamers See Through Fear

Words for Tomorrow...

Journeying Through Fear

I was scared that this person would misunderstand

my character if I shared my true desire with them

I had to remind myself that I couldn't fall victim to

the fear that stopped me from sharing my truth

And so, I wrote

I wrote the things I was too scared to say out loud

I wrote as if I knew they were going to read every

poem

I painted my desire the only way I knew how...

For Tomorrow

Your words float off your lips and echo through my
body

I awake and your lyrics flood my mind, they upwell
my sea of thoughts

The essence of you made my pen move across the
paper

You awoke the spirit that allowed my fear to
dissipate

I see your life through your music
I've met you through your cadence

You seem to match my energy precisely

We see the ins and outs of humanity
We understand that fear comes from within

We have the same passion for life,
creating, sharing, learning

We are of the same mind, the same spirit
Our devotion to life is contagious

Come,
Come join me
Come create realities with me

We can learn each other and the world around us

You can hypnotize me and I can mesmerize you

But until then,

I await the tomorrow that brings you to me

Getting Lost In Tomorrow

I'll tell you that it feels right to imagine loving you
You'll smile and pull me towards you

I'll tell you that this wine gets me going
You'll laugh and pour me another glass

Your arms will wrap around my waist and we'll
dance, we'll dance like it's the only thing we were
meant to do

I'll ask you what you think about my desire for all
and you'll say to me

*It's magnificent, it's proof that your capacity to love
is infinite*

If Tomorrow Was Real

If you were real,
I'd cop us some girl scout cookies and we'd have
ourselves a damn good time

If you were real,
I'd tell you that your art makes me feel everything
and nothing all at the same time

If you were real,
I'd play you the songs that guided me along my
journey and you would see that music means the
same thing to both of us

If you were real I'd tell you that,

The Essence Of You Helped Me Journey Through
My Fear

Finally Living Fearlessly...

Freedom From Fear

It took a long time for me to love the way I was

destined to move through this world

There's no way I'm going to limit myself now

The only one who can stop me, is me

Fearless is the way I choose to live...

Letter To Myself

Never apologize for being you
Do not let others bully you into invalidating your
own feelings

Love yourself entirely
Be addicted to yourself

You are the only thing you can control

What others do, whether it is good or bad, is not
because of you

Trust that everything you think, feel, and do
matters

You are kind
You are beautiful
You are intelligent

Everything You Need Lies Within

A Lifetime of Love

A life of mountains and valleys,
we moved with the wind

Road trips across the country,
we journeyed with a purpose

Car rides to the chiropractor,
we sung along with Travis Scott

Family dinners that lasted hours,
we shared laughs across the table

A lifetime of loving one another,
A lifetime spent reinventing what it means to be a
family

I am blessed because

I Only Ever Had To Be Me To Be Loved

EARTH

The wind blows to give us a cool breeze on the
days that seem to hot to bear

The rain falls to give us water so our bodies can be
replenished

The flowers bloom to give us an abundance of
colors so we're reminded to live a radiant life

This beauty is normalized so we forget to admire
its existence

We forget to appreciate the beauty that we cannot
control

May We Always Give Back More Than We Take

TECHNOLOGY

We rely so much on it,

it controls everyday life

It is not just our phones,

it is our cars, our weapons

Technology is not the end, it is only the beginning

Whether it destroys or unites is up to us

Let Us Choose Wisely

Good Ole Social Media

Your life has become a series of likes and
comments

Trends fuel your actions while your opinions are
recycled

You spend more time scrolling on your phone then
you do with your family

You live for your followers instead of living for
yourself

YOU NEED TO WAKE UP

Don't you see that this dependency is dangerous?

I'm not saying you need to get rid of social media
And I'm not saying all its qualities are bad

All I'm saying is that you must

Be Mindful Of The Power You Give To The Virtual
World Instead Of To Yourself

BLACK ICE

I used to write about you with anger..

a little resentment here, a little resentment there

I reflect with a smile because I get it now..

you were just doing what you thought was best

You were bound by society and fear..

you didn't know any better

I Could Never Blame You For Your Humanness

The Journey of Life

Life is really just a series of revelations

Everyone you come across is essential to your
growth
They either teach you a lesson or they become a
friend

Ensure that those you hold close have the same
desires as you, otherwise you'll be mislead

Understand that we are all here contributing to the
human condition

You could only ever be you, so trust in your
abilities

Everything happens for a reason no matter what
you believe in

There Is Purpose In Everything
You Just Have To Find It

HOW TO FIND YOUR PEOPLE

You must be your truest self,
Your rawest and most authentic self

You will see that you were put on this planet for a
reason, you will see that your capabilities are
endless

Never forget,

You Get Back What You Give To The World

To Be Unstoppable

You are not what you see
You are the sun rising in the day and the the stars
shining at night

You are not the world around you
You are the moon's gravitational pull, shifting
waves and forming tides

You are not the posts you read or the likes you
depend on
You are a creator of realities

Free yourself from the barriers of society
You are bound to nothing as long as you see
through the facade

Let go of fear and let your imagination run wild
Search for your truth and when you find it, share it
with the world

You Will Find You Are Unstoppable

Genuinely, Genuine

To be me is beautiful

To be an artist is magical

To exist is prevalent

I speak and love transcends

I write and reality is painted

I listen and I see the nuances of life

I'm free from the barriers of reality

I'm living a boundless life

I am living

Genuinely, Genuine

Closing Thoughts

I used to be afraid to call myself a writer. I didn't allow myself to speak the things I dreamt about into existence. If writing was just a hobby, then I wouldn't have to step out of my comfort zone.

Eventually, I grew tired of being stuck in a cycle of falsehood. I grew tired of limiting my existence. And so, I wrote about my experiences in the rawest way possible. I didn't sugarcoat the fear or the anxiety and I was unapologetic about my love and happiness. Now, I understand that my desires should not be feared, they should fuel my existence. I must put aside my fear, so I can live a boundless life.

Of course, that is easier said than done. Living fearlessly is something I'm still learning how to do. Every day I have to remind myself to be kind to my mind. I have to remind myself to speak with a purpose and to do what feeds my soul. I often find myself in situations where I can either conform to society or I can be myself. Every time, I choose to be me.

This book is a documentation of my seventeen years of existence. By composing this book, I am sharing a series of experiences I had over the course of my life. With these experiences came revelations that brought me to this point in my life. The biggest revelation I had was the importance of unlocking human potential. I believe that everyone has a purpose on this planet. We are all capable of turning the things we imagine into reality. This book is my way of bringing everything I've imagined to life. When I write, I'm freeing myself from the limitations of the past, future, and present. I'm freeing myself from myself.

There is still so much to do and so much to learn, this book is only the beginning. Thank you for joining me along my journey. Never forget that you are changing the world just by existing. May you live well and live genuinely!

Made in the USA
Monee, IL
30 August 2020